Arthur
in London

For Dom, Anouck and Thibaut, who light up my way, day after day.
For Laura, Tibor and Antoine: travel as soon as you have the opportunity to do so, there is nothing on earth that provides better memories.
For all of those who liked Arthur in Geneva.

This is Arthur's second travel adventure. The first, also published by Grace Note Publications, is *Arthur in Geneva* (*Arthur à Genève*)
www.arthurvoyage.ch

Arthur in London
English translation of *Arthur à Londres*
First edition, 2016 by Grace Note Publications.
Grange of Locherlour, Ochtertyre, PH7 4JS
Scotland, UK

www.gracenotepublications.co.uk
books@gracenotereading.co.uk
www.arthurvoyage.ch

ISBN 978-1-907676-82-6 [English]
ISBN 978-1-907676-74-1 [French]

Original text©Caroline Ferrero Menut, 2016
Illustrations©Nicole Devals, 2016
Translation©Grace Note Publications, 2016

Translation, and edited by
Paul Malgrati, Eberhard Bort and Susy Macaulay

All rights reserved

A catalogue record for this book is available from the British Library

Arthur
in London

Caroline Ferrero Menut

Illustrator Nicole Devals

Travelling had always been my dream; and when I realised I had an amazing secret power to travel in my dreams, I had only one thought: when would it happen again? And where would it take me? Yet it all turned out very differently from how I imagined…

Chapter 1
Tess

A GIRL HAD ARRIVED FOR THE SUMMER at the farm next door. She was a lot taller than me and at least seven years older. You might have taken her for a grown-up, but she spoke and played like a child.

She was called Tess, a name I had never heard before. The name suited her, it was sweet and pretty, just like her.

Tess helped our neighbours; she cleaned, looked after the children and sometimes did a bit farm work.

I had been secretly observing her for a while. She smiled mischievously all the time, and was always playing with her long, bright hair, sometimes gathering it on top of her head, in a kind of bun. I found that so cool.

But what I found most charming about her and loved straight away, was her accent. Sometimes in the evening before falling asleep, I closed my eyes and thought again of her voice. It made me smile immediately. I had no idea why, and I began to wonder if I hadn't become a little bit soft in the head.

I was always very shy when I wanted to speak to her, but one day I plucked up all my courage and asked her:

"Where do you come from, Tess? You're so different from the girls I see at school."

"I was born and grew up in London, in England, but I left my country several years ago."

"And what's England like?"

"Well I'm a bit nostalgic, I long to see London again, it's a beautiful city, so full of life. But let's talk about something else, otherwise I might look sad today"

I could sense the shaking in her voice, and she started shivering. Then all of a sudden I said blushing:

"Well, as soon as I get a bit of money, I will take you back to see London, and the whole of England if you want."

She smiled back:

"I can't believe it, you're still a kid and you already know how to talk to a woman."

Then she grabbed a bucket of water and ran at me, pretending she was going to throw it all over me. I ran away as fast as I could and I heard her burst out laughing. Oh that laugh, it was the sweetest music in the world.

Chapter 2
The Departure

T̲h̲e̲ ̲s̲h̲o̲r̲t̲ ̲c̲h̲a̲s̲e̲ left me out of breath. I sat under a big oak and closed my eyes, thinking how lovely Tess was.

The breeze was soft and smelled of the countryside. I had drifted into sleep when a voice, shouting my name, woke me up all of a sudden.

"Arthur, ARTHUR, this is no time to sleep, come and see this, it's wonderful, incredible, awesome, fantastic."

I opened one eye, and there was Tess, standing in front of me with a bright smile and a gleam in her eye I hadn't noticed before.

"Look around, you must be a magician, here we are, in my city."

I couldn't understand why she was so excited, and I don't like noise when I wake up, so I answered her grumpily:

"I don't understand a word you're saying, Tess, leave me alone."

But she insisted: "Poor thing, open your eyes, this is no time to be sleeping."

I looked around me. There were a lot of people. I spotted some huge billboards with multi-coloured lights that looked like television screens, it was exciting. I was sitting next to a big fountain with a winged angel at the top of it carrying a bow. It looked like Cupid, the angel who shoots arrows at people so that they fall in love.

I couldn't believe it. Where had I landed? I said hesitantly:

"But where are we?" Tess answered: "In Piccadilly Circus, London, England, my friend, just like you said, you did it."

"Unbelievable." I was baffled, but then it dawned on me: I was travelling again and, even better, Tess was my guide. Who would have thought this could ever happen? It was truly magic.

Tess said brightly:

"Let's not waste time. I'm so happy, come on, I'm going to give you a tour of the city. You can't come all the way here without seeing all the brilliant things from my childhood memories."

She didn't know it, but I would have followed her to the other side of the world if she had asked.

Chapter 3
Aventure Time

We ran down a never-ending street also called Piccadilly, just like the square where I had woken up, and arrived at a lovely park. Tess told me that it was called Green Park, which I found funny.

"I'm taking you to the Queen of England's palace. You know – she's called Elizabeth; she's in every magazine and on television. She always wears beautiful hats. Oh, I forgot, you don't watch television and don't read newspapers. Well that's even better, I'm going to teach you everything."

We came to a big square, at the end of which stood a long, striking building made of pale stones, with two rows of identical windows on either side of the middle entrance. The path to get inside the building was protected by railings.

"This is Buckingham Palace, where our Queen lives. It's beautiful, don't you think? But there's something really funny. See the guards over there?"

"Those two lads all in red with weird hats that look a bit like giant teddy bears?"

"Exactly. And, by the way, their hats are made of real bearskin.

"Animal rights activists don't like it. They want them replaced with imitations. But, there is something odd about these guards you know: they have to guard the Queen's palace without saying a word and stand stock still except for their rounds. Can you imagine that? Standing for hours on the spot without talking? I'd find that impossible."

She went up to one of them and said:

"Hey, Mister Queen's Guard, are you not too warm with that big black bearskin hat on your head?"

I was taken aback.

"Are you crazy? You'll get locked up, Tess!"

"Not at all, you can ask him whatever you want, he won't answer or move. They're highly-trained and truly disciplined soldiers."

I had indeed noticed that the guard hadn't moved, and that he didn't even look bothered. I hesitated for a moment and with a slight blush, said to the guard:

"Look, Mister, you've got a huge stain on your trousers."

Tess and I roared with laughter, like kids, until our bellies ached and tears were running down my face. The guard didn't even smile. He remained perfectly immobile and expressionless. Those guards are true professionals.

"The tour continues. We're going to see the most famous bell in the world."

"A bell! But our farm is already ringing with them."

She shook her head as if she thought I was a fool, and took my hand. My heart started pounding in my chest.

Tess was really amazing, like a girl from a fairy tale. I was sure they didn't exist in real life, and yet I had met one – me, Arthur, the little country boy.

Tess interrupted my daydream.

"Look at this tower. It's a clock tower. The bell is right at the top. It's called Big Ben."

"Where does that name come from?"

"We don't really know. Some people say it's the name of the engineer who was behind the building of this tower: his name was Benjamin, and he was quite chubby, therefore the name Big Ben. Others say it's in memory of a champion boxer called Ben: he beat the defending champion in an incredible fight in the year the bell was made."

"So, how do you like the bell?"

"I like everything when I'm with you… and I like the tales you tell."

"We haven't even started yet; now I'm taking you to an exceptional bridge."

"Right with you, Tess."

"We're going to take the Tube."

I followed her down steps leading below the street, and we came to a sort of underground station with huge tunnels and trains that took people from one side of London to the other. This town is like a giant Swiss cheese with holes and tunnels everywhere, I thought. It has a truly secret life, hidden from people on the surface.

We made several stops and when we finally came back up into daylight, we walked towards a wide river, crossed by a bridge running between two huge stone towers, with iron or steel cables spanning the whole length of it.

"I visited this bridge with my school, you know, and our teacher told us all about its history. You see, at that time, there weren't many ways to cross the Thames."

"The Thames?"

"Yes, that's the name of the river in front of you. So, to continue – people wanted to build a new bridge to make it easier to cross from one side to the other. But boats, which came from all over the world to unload their goods, had to be able to pass under the bridge. At the same time, the bridge had to be strong enough so that any type of vehicle could use it. From 1850 onwards, architects drew up plans, more than fifty different ones I think, and it was only thirty-six years later that the actual construction started. Can you imagine? Thirty-six years to design a bridge! And do you know how long it took to build it?"

"Erm, a few years?"

"Eight years, my friend."

"It's really beautiful when the bridge opens to let boats pass, but I don't know if that's going to happen today. Do you want to climb up the tower to have a great view?"

"No offence, Tess, but I'm really hungry now, and a bit tired."

"Oh you young people, only thinking about your stomach," she said, sounding slightly annoyed.

Chapter 4
Lunch Time!

"All right, if you want to eat, I'm taking you to China."

"To China? But that's really too far away."

"Always negative, aren't you? You'll see. And as you're tired, let's take a double-decker."

Before I could even try to understand, she had jumped onto a two-storey bus. I followed her without thinking, and we took seats on the upper deck.

"Wow, this bus is amazing, and what a view!"

"Ah, Monsieur is waking up a bit," she said with a grin. "It's true, these buses are really cool, they're part of London life and they're on every postcard, they've become a symbol of the city."

We fell silent and watched houses, people and shops roll by. Tess ran her hand through my hair. I couldn't have imagined such happiness in my wildest dreams.

"Come on, everybody off, we're here."

On getting off the bus, we found ourselves in a strange place. All the houses, shops and restaurants had indeed a Chinese vibe. I had often looked at books about China in the school library and I had kept all the pictures in my head: small and low houses, red wood, lamps made of paper like balloons. All of that was here, and also there were Chinese people all over the place.

"Where are we? Have we left England?"

"No, silly, it's the Chinese neighbourhood, Soho, have you never heard of it?"

"I don't think so."

"As a lot of Chinese people live in London, they've come together little by little over time and formed their own neighbourhood to recreate the atmosphere of their country. There are loads of Chinese restaurants, and grocery shops where people can buy any Chinese specialities they might need to cook their favourite meals at home. I've a friend who's a cook and who makes the best Lacquered Peking Duck you will ever taste. Let's go."

"A duck with lacquer on it? That can't be very good, can it?"

"You'll see – it's a very sophisticated Chinese speciality."

I met her friend, who greeted us with a broad smile. He was obviously very happy to see Tess again. Although I was a bit worried about eating this lacquered duck, I must say I really enjoyed it. It tasted like good chicken but with a firmer texture, and the sauce was delicious. We felt so good to be together, far from home, in this city that Tess loved so much. She was glowing and seemed to me even more beautiful than usual.

"Come on, we're going to get a dessert which is a speciality from home, you'll love it."

"Alright! I'm up for it, I love desserts."

We walked for a bit, and she bought two strange-looking big chocolate madeleines called 'muffins', with loads of chocolate chips inside. They were gorgeous, I loved them and asked Tess if she could bake some at home or give the recipe to my mum so that we could make it together.

"Of course, then every time you eat them you'll think of me."

Tess didn't know it, but I knew I didn't need to eat a muffin to think of her. Had this awesome girl bewitched me?

"Let's eat the muffins on the pavement at Covent Garden. There are always very enjoyable shows going on there, you'll see."

Chapter 5
The Hat

We reached a sort of covered market where many artisans were selling their wares. We saw two musicians performing, and we sat on the ground to listen to them. There were many people, young and old, and everyone seemed happy to be there.

Some were just listening, others were clapping to the beat, and some were even dancing. It was fun. A little further away, acrobats were putting on a show, and the crowd gathered around them was so big that it was difficult to see them. People were laughing. I could have stayed there for days.

I leaned over to thank Tess for taking me there, but I noticed with dismay that she was no longer sitting next to me. She had disappeared.

I leapt up and thankfully spotted her not too far away at a stall, trying on a hat. It suited her so well that it looked like it had been designed for her, and I do have some knowledge as to what suits a girl.

She checked herself in the mirror the seller was holding in front of her, tilting her head to one side.

I think it is at that precise moment that I eventually understood what was happening to me: I had fallen in love with Tess. Me, Arthur, I was IN LOVE.

I went closer to her and gently asked: "Do you like that hat?"

"Oh yes, it's great, it looks like it's been specially made for me." Confident, and without thinking, I asked the stallholder:

"Sir, how much is this hat?"

"Twenty pounds, young man."

I went all red in the face. I didn't have any money and I didn't even know how much "one-pound" was actually worth.

He looked at me, smiling like someone who had experienced this kind of situation, and he whispered to me:

"I really like your belt, I'll swap it for the hat."

"Oh, really? That's great, you're really kind, Sir."

He gave me a wink as I walked over to Tess who was standing a bit further away.

"Take it; it's yours, so that you can be happy on rainy days, or on days you feel lonely, when I won't be around."

She looked gravely at me.

"You're still a little man, but you're so adorable. Thank you, from all my heart. You're so sensitive, so attentive. Really, Arthur, a big thank-you to you."

I was over the moon.

Chapter 6
The End of our Afternoon

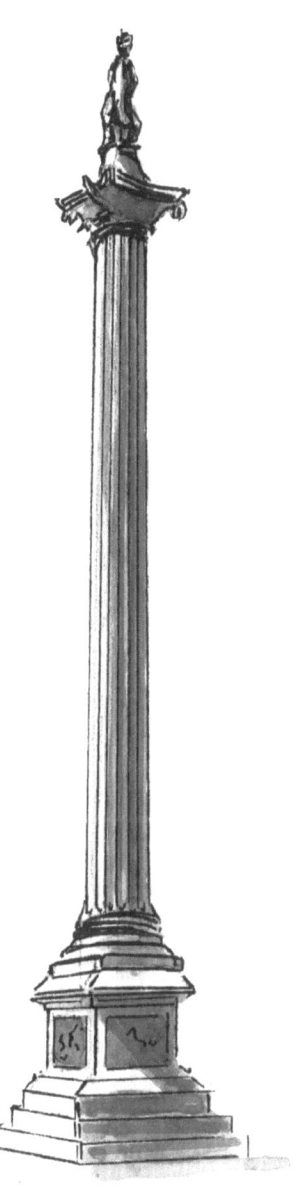

"I still have to show you one place that I love, with its fountains, pigeons and lions, I'm sure you'll love it too."

"Lions, here, in London, in the middle of the city?"

"Yes, come on Arthur, you'll see."

We walked quietly for a few moments until we came to a very big square with a huge column, on the top of which was perched a statue of a man.

"Tess, what on earth is that bloke doing up there?"

"It's NELSON, the great English admiral. You know, the one who won the famous naval battle of TRAFALGAR against the French and the Spanish, after he had captured twenty ships of theirs without losing a single English one. This place was created in commemoration of all that, and it bears the name of the battle: TRAFALGAR square."

I looked around: the square was an impressive size. We were at the upper end of it, and there were big stone steps leading down to four massive lions, made of black stone.

"I understand about the lions now, they're statues. They're superb. Come on, let's say hello to the wild beasts."

"Yes I'm fond of this place but the sun is going down and I would still like to show you what the city did to celebrate the Millennium, so let's walk a bit more."

We walked in silence; both of us were quite tired. On the other side of the Thames, I saw a gigantic Ferris wheel, at least 300 feet high.

"A Ferris wheel…"

"Yes, it's the 'London Eye'. Londoners wanted to celebrate the turn of the millennium by building something that would leave a lasting legacy and the City just fell for this Ferris wheel, which can be seen from miles away. You can even see it from a plane. But above all, it gives a wonderful view of my London. Come on, let's take a ride."

We took our seats and rose into the air like birds. The sun was setting, lighting up the sky with pink. I could see the Thames, the city of London; it was as beautiful as a film. Tess was smiling from ear to ear and she put her head on my shoulder.

I had never been so happy in my whole life. I closed my eyes and let myself fill to the brim with happiness.

"Arthur, Arthur, what are you doing?"

I opened my eyes and amazingly, I was lying under the big oak tree at home and Tess was standing in front of me.

"Have we just got back from London?" I asked, still half asleep.

"What on earth are you talking about? Have you got sunstroke? Up you get and hurry home, your parents are going to worry, you've been here for hours."

I got up and watched her walking away. Could it be true? I really had been to London. All those memories I had. I had eaten that Lacquered Peking Duck. Tess and I had really experienced all these extraordinary moments...

I watched her walking away. On her head was the beautiful hat I had bought her at Covent Garden. I cried out:

"Just a minute Tess, your hat, where did you get it?"

"I can't remember and I don't know why, whenever I wear it, be it rainy, windy or sunny, I'm HAPPYYYYY. That's why I never take it off."

This left me wondering... but suddenly I understood: that was it, I had been on my travels again, it was my second voyage and, moreover, with Tess. It was the most beautiful present life could have given me. Tess and I, travelling together on our own.

I ran home and asked my mother if I could borrow our camera.

"What do you want it for?"

"It's for school, I have to take pictures."

She handed it over to me, shaking her head to show she didn't believe me at all.

I ran back to Tess's farm and there, from a well-hidden spot, I managed to take a picture of her with her lovely hat, so that I could keep it in my box of travel souvenirs.

That night I went to bed and looked at my box with the key to Geneva and the picture of Tess in London in it.

I couldn't help wondering when I would travel again, and where? Everything had been so perfect so far, and it was hard to imagine how I would ever be so happy again in future.

But I was wide of the mark. My next adventure would have many more surprises in store for me.

THE END

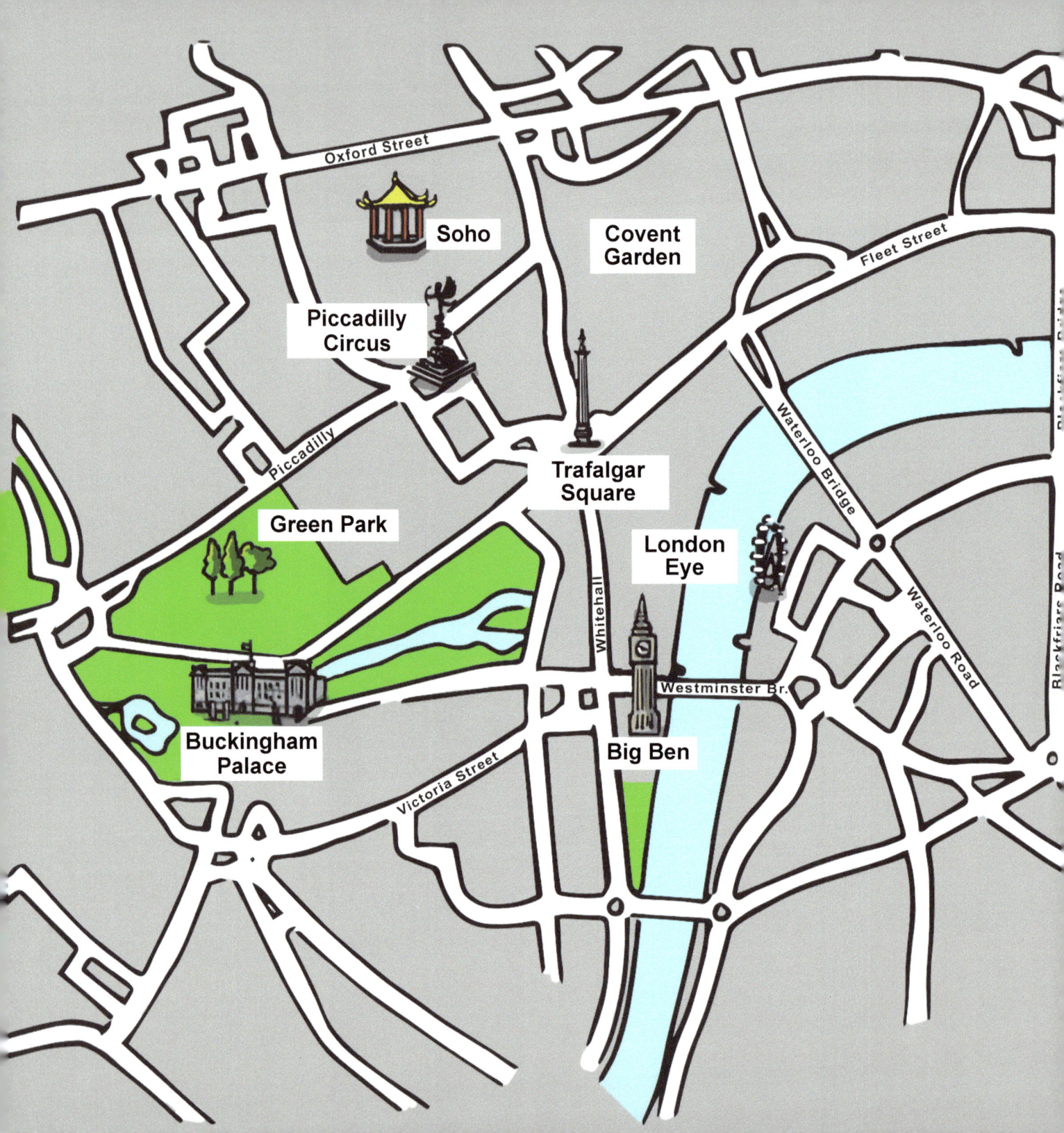

Arthur in London

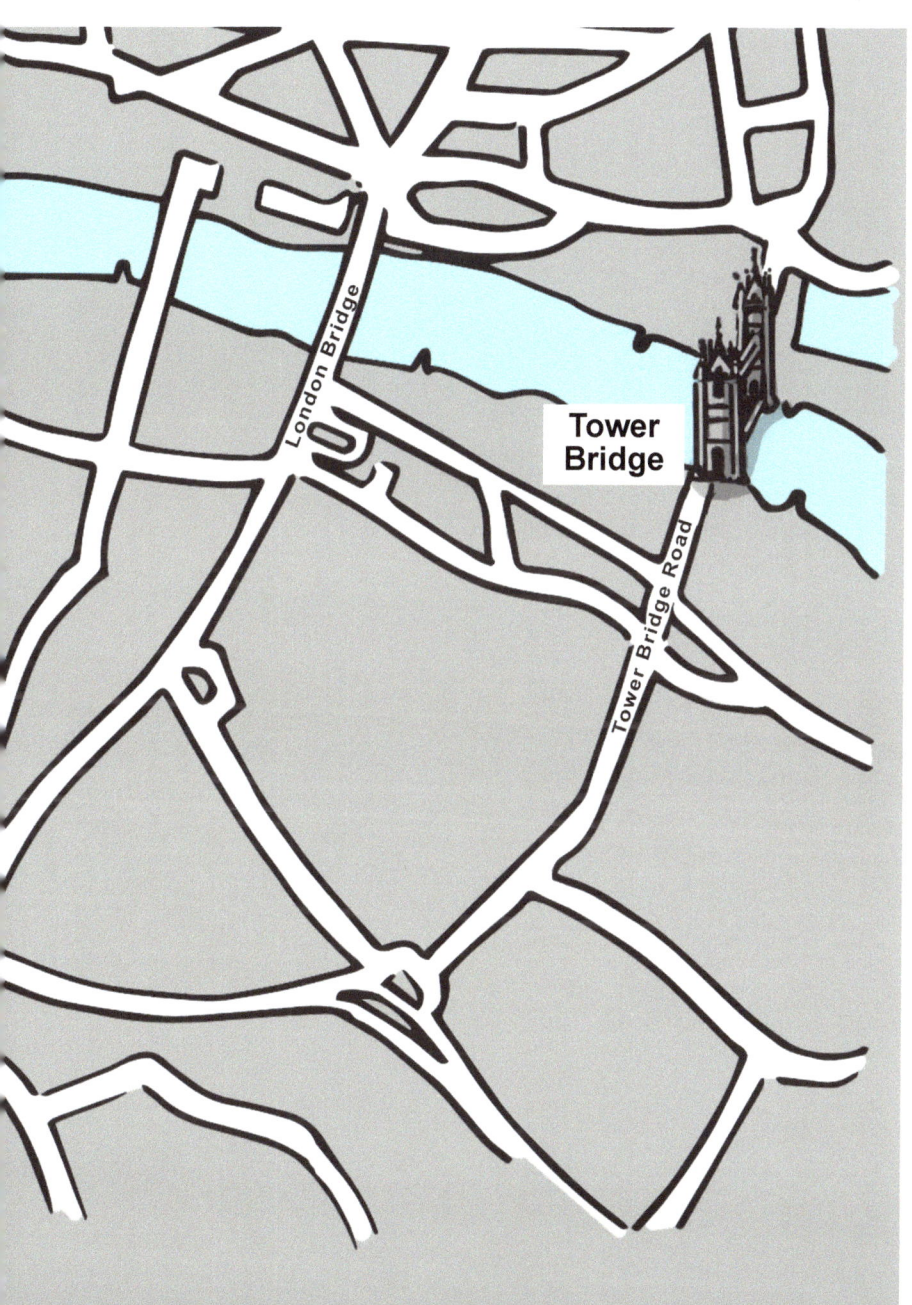

A note about the Author

CAROLINE FERRERO MENUT
I have always been fascinated by how easily children learn as well as by their curiosity for everything that surrounds them. As a mother and as a travel enthusiast, I made up fun stories to encourage our children to discover new places with us, and it has worked beyond my expectations. We have visited countless villages, cities and countries, near and far, in the footsteps of imaginary characters specially invented for the occasion, all this with a real enthusiasm, joy and excitement. Working as a lawyer, I am used to writing and I wanted, through the publication of the adventures of *Arthur in Geneva* and *Arthur in London*, to share with other children the great pleasure of broadening one's horizons.

A note about the Illustrator

NICOLE DEVALS
Since my early childhood drawing has been a wonderful means of expression for me. Thanks to the experience gained during my student years at the Ecole Emile Cohl, in Lyon, and from all those hours spent drawing and sketching, I am now lucky enough to be able to make a living from my passion, putting my skills at the service of educational and nature conservation associations as well as others who promote values close to my heart. I take a lot of pleasure in illustrating children's stories and Arthur's adventures – *Arthur in Geneva* and *Arthur in London* – are of particular interest to me, as they demand a documentary, technical style of drawing, but also a strong emotional approach.

www.ingramcontent.com/pod-product-compliance
Lightning Source LLC
Chambersburg PA
CBHW060758090426
42736CB00002B/76